# GREEN WHALES

*Lia Romeo*

**BROADWAY PLAY PUBLISHING INC**
New York
www.broadwayplaypublishing.com
info@broadwayplaypublishing.com

GREEN WHALES
© Copyright 2018 Lia Romeo

Cover art courtesy of Forward Flux Productions. Photo by Joe Moore.

First edition: December 2018
I S B N: 978-0-88145-806-0

Book design: Marie Donovan
Page make-up: Adobe InDesign
Typeface: Palatino

GREEN WHALES had its world premiere on 5 March 2010, presented by Unicorn Theatre (Artistic Director, Cynthia Levin) in collaboration with University of Missouri, Kansas City Theatre. The cast and creative contributors were:

KAREN WILSON...................................................... Anna Safar
JOANNA WILSON...................................... Vanessa Severo
RAY PRATT .............................................. Darren Kennedy
IAN MILTON ......................................................Dean Vivian

*Director* ......................................................... Cynthia Levin
*Stage manager* ................................................Tanya Brown
*Technical director* ...........................................James Keith
*Scenic designer* ............................................. Tabitha Pease
*Lighting designer* ......................................... Latrice Lovett
*Sound designer* ....................................Benjamin G Stickels
*Costume designer* ........................................ Renee Garcia
*Properties designer* ............................... David Hawkinson
*Dramaturg* ...................................................... Erin DeSeure

# CHARACTERS & SETTING

KAREN WILSON, *38, but looks like she's in her early teens*
JOANNA WILSON, *36*
RAY PRATT, *35*
IAN MILTON, *40*

*Place: Paradise, New Jersey.*

*Time: The present, or something like it.*

## Scene 1

(JOANNA's *kitchen.* KAREN, *dressed in black, is sitting at the kitchen table. There is a drink in front of her, and a bottle of vodka, along with another empty glass, across the table. As lights come up, we hear the sound of vomiting from the bathroom offstage.*)

KAREN: Are you all right?

(*The vomiting pauses for a moment...then resumes with renewed vigor. After another moment,* JOANNA *enters, dressed in black and wiping her mouth.*)

JOANNA: I'm fine. (*She picks up the vodka and pours some into her glass.*)

KAREN: You're having another drink?

JOANNA: Why not?

KAREN: Um. Because you just threw up after drinking half of that bottle.

JOANNA: Right, I know, so now it's all out of my system. You want some more?

KAREN: No, I'm all right, I'm going to go to bed in a minute.

JOANNA: Have another drink with me first.

KAREN: No, I don't want—

JOANNA: Please? Just one more? I really don't feel like being alone right now.

KAREN: Okay.

(JOANNA *pours more vodka into* KAREN'*s glass.*)

JOANNA: To Mom.

KAREN: May she rest in peace.

JOANNA: That, or burn in hell.

KAREN: Haven't you heard the saying—we shouldn't speak ill of the dead?

JOANNA: Is that the saying? 'Cause I thought it was that we shouldn't speak ill of the dead *unless* the dead was a miserable bitch.

KAREN: Jo…

JOANNA: I was meeting Ray for lunch last week, and I wore my snakeskin sandals—the pink ones—and then afterwards I went over to the hospital. The sores in her mouth were so bad she could hardly talk, but when I came in she looked me up and down and she said—in that raspy, croaking voice, she said—"You look like a two dollar whore. And the dollar's weak right now."

KAREN: That's terrible.

JOANNA: I think it was the last thing she ever said to me.
I'm glad you came. I couldn't have handled all this alone.

KAREN: I know.

*(Beat)*

JOANNA: So now that the funeral's over…how long do you think you're going to stay?

KAREN: I don't know. I'll probably head back in a few days.

JOANNA: Oh—that soon?

KAREN: When she got diagnosed it seemed like it would be so quick, but I've been here what—almost two months already.

JOANNA: Yeah, I know, but I was hoping you'd stay another week or two. It's so nice having you here.

KAREN: Yeah—you may think so, but I'm pretty sure Ray doesn't. Speaking of which...

JOANNA: I told you, he had to work.

KAREN: And that's more important than being there for your mother's funeral?

JOANNA: Well, you know, he's trying to make detective...

KAREN: He could have taken the afternoon off.

JOANNA: I know. I'm sure he would have, if I'd asked. But it's not like they were exactly close. (*She reaches for the vodka again.*)

KAREN: I thought you were just having one more.

JOANNA: I'm quitting. Cold turkey. Starting tomorrow. It was just sort of an awful afternoon.

KAREN: Did you think it was going to be fun?

JOANNA: No, of course not...but I didn't think it was going to be so...

KAREN: What?

JOANNA: I mean, I always pictured my funeral with lots of friends and loved ones gathered around, singing songs and telling stories and fucking each other in the bathroom—all that life-affirming stuff. But what if it's not like that at all? What if it's a big empty room and a preacher who can't even say my name right?

KAREN: Yeah. I would have thought at least Aunt Sally would come.

JOANNA: I don't think they've spoken in almost ten years. Since the time we all went to Aunt Sally's for Thanksgiving—

KAREN: Oh yeah, and Mom threw the turkey at her head.

JOANNA: Yeah.

(KAREN *and* JOANNA *sigh, drink.*)

JOANNA: I just don't want to die alone, you know?

KAREN: I think you're a little young to be worrying about that.

JOANNA: No, you know what I read the other day? Forty year old single women have better odds of being in a terrorist attack than they do of ever getting married.

KAREN: What?

JOANNA: Yeah.

KAREN: Well, that's probably because a lot of them don't want to get married.

JOANNA: I mean, that's true, but I want to get married. Don't you?

KAREN: I don't know.

JOANNA: Cause you know, if you do…

KAREN: I don't know if I do.

JOANNA: Okay, but you're thirty-eight, and you're not even dating.

Are you?

KAREN: No.

JOANNA: And last time I checked, that was sort of a prerequisite. Unless you wanted an arranged marriage, and seeing as Mom's dead and we haven't seen Dad in, I don't know, thirty years, it's sort of unlikely that they'll be setting one up.

KAREN: Yeah, well, I'm not very good at dating. I have this disease, in case you haven't noticed.

JOANNA: Turner Syndrome is not a disease. It's a chromosomal condition.

I'm a really good matchmaker. You know my friend Lisa? I set her up with the guy she wound up marrying.

KAREN: Wasn't that guy a coke dealer?

JOANNA: Well, yeah, they're divorced now. But they had a really great six months.

KAREN: Did I ever tell you what happened with the last guy I got set up with?

JOANNA: No…

KAREN: It was maybe a year ago—back in Chicago. His name was Nick—he worked with my friend Carla. And I guess she didn't tell him about…what was wrong with me, 'cause as soon as he saw me he just got this…weird…. But he was pretty lonely, I guess, and so was I, because we had a few drinks and the next thing you know we ended up in bed together.

JOANNA: *(Excited)* Really?

KAREN: Yeah. And then once we were done he started crying, and said it made him feel like he was molesting a twelve year old.

JOANNA: Oh. Wow.

KAREN: Yeah. I haven't gone out with anybody since then.

(JOANNA *pours herself more vodka. She proffers the bottle to* KAREN. KAREN *pours herself more vodka as well. They drink in silence for a moment.*)

JOANNA: You know what, though…there are a lot of men who like that kind of thing.

KAREN: What, molesting twelve year olds?

JOANNA: Yeah.

KAREN: You mean pedophiles?

JOANNA: Yeah…

KAREN: You think I should date pedophiles?
I don't want to date pedophiles!

JOANNA: Why not?

KAREN: Because they have sex with children!

JOANNA: But if they were having sex with you, they *wouldn't* be having sex with children. It's kind of like you'd be doing a public service.

KAREN: How drunk *are* you?

JOANNA: I'm really drunk. But you know, it'd be easy to meet them.

KAREN: Oh yeah?

JOANNA: They're all on the sex offender registry. There's probably three or four right in this neighborhood.

KAREN: Great!

JOANNA: Want to look?

KAREN: No!

JOANNA: I do. *(She begins typing on her phone.)* National Sex Offender Registry…

KAREN: Jo…

JOANNA: Find sex offenders in your area…

KAREN: Jo, quit it.

JOANNA: Oh, look! He's cute.

*(KAREN leans over to look.)*

KAREN: He was arrested for exposing himself to an eight year old!

JOANNA: Oh yeah…

KAREN: Twice!

*(Beat)*

JOANNA: What about this one? Statutory rape—that's good—he was nineteen and he did it with a fifteen year old.

KAREN: If he was nineteen and he did it with a fifteen year old, he's probably not really a pedophile.

JOANNA: That's true.
Or how about this one? He's kind of funny looking—but look here—crossed state lines with the intention of having sex with a twelve year old…boy, never mind…

KAREN: Okay, you know what? You can stay up all night looking at pedophiles if you want to, but I'm going to bed.

JOANNA: No, wait. I have another idea. *(She begins typing again.)*

KAREN: What are you doing?

JOANNA: Have you ever met anyone online?

KAREN: I was on Match for a little while. But then they made me take down my picture, because they said they weren't allowed to have pictures of children, and if you don't have a picture then everyone figures you're ugly and they don't send you any messages.

JOANNA: What about chat rooms? Have you ever spent any time in any of those?

*(KAREN shakes her head.)*

JOANNA: Oh, they're fun. They're like little online communities full of people with similar interests.

KAREN: Like philosophy?

JOANNA: Yeah. Kind of like that. *(She begins typing again.)* So, first we'll set you up with a profile—

KAREN: No—I don't want a profile—

JOANNA: Let's see. Height, four feet, ten inches. Weight…eighty-five pounds?

(KAREN *nods.*)

JOANNA: Hair, brown, eyes, brown. Age… *(She studies* KAREN *for a moment.)* Fourteen.

KAREN: *Fourteen?*

JOANNA: Everyone lies about their age online. I was twenty-five on eHarmony for at least five years.

KAREN: I'm a middle-aged woman, Jo!

JOANNA: You need a screen name. How about…Sexyjuniorhighcheerleader. *(Reading)* "Sexyjuniorhighcheerleader is taken. Would you like Sexyjuniorhighcheerleader5613?"

KAREN: There are 5,612 other sexy junior high cheerleaders on the internet?

JOANNA: I'm surprised there aren't more than that, actually. *(She presses enter, then, reading)* "Congratulations, you have created a profile…would you like to log into one of our chat rooms?" Let's see… *(She scrolls down)* "Luscious Lesbians"…no. "Bisexual Biker Boys"…no. "Tie Me Up and Shit On My Chest"…

KAREN: Ew!

JOANNA: No. "I Heart Older Men." Hmm. That might work.

(JOANNA *presses enter. For a moment, nothing happens. Then the phone beeps. Reading)*

JOANNA: You have received an instant message from: MonsterCock23. Would you like to accept it?

KAREN: No.

JOANNA: Yeah you would. *(She clicks, then, reading)* "I have a 14 inch cock."

KAREN: Yeah, right.

JOANNA: *(Typing)* "Me too."

*(The phone beeps. Reading)*

JOANNA: MonsterCock23 has logged off.

*(The phone beeps again. Reading)*

JOANNA: "You have received an instant message from: SuperSchlong17. Would you like to accept it?"

KAREN: No!

*(The phone beeps again.)*

JOANNA: "You have received an instant message from"—hey, pookie!

*(JOANNA puts her phone down quickly as RAY enters, wearing a policeman's uniform. He holds a bouquet.)*

RAY: Hey, tootsie roll. Hi, Karen.

*(RAY hands JOANNA the flowers.)*

RAY: I'm sorry I had to miss the funeral. I brought you these.

JOANNA: Pookie, that's so sweet! *(She opens the card.)* Who's Claire?

RAY: Oh, sorry. I got 'em off a dead guy. Got rear-ended by a semi on his way home to give them to his wife.

JOANNA: Oh. *(She drinks.)*

RAY: I thought you were going to quit.

JOANNA: I am. Tomorrow. You want some?

RAY: I'll have a beer. *(He crosses to the fridge and takes out a beer.)* So…Karen…now that the funeral's over—how long do you think you're going to stay?

KAREN: I'll probably head back in a few days.

RAY: Oh—that long?

JOANNA: Pookie…

KAREN: Um. Okay, I really am going to go to bed.

JOANNA: No, don't. We've still got all this vodka to get through.

KAREN: You're not seriously going to drink that all tonight.

JOANNA: I'm quitting. I want to get it out of the house.

KAREN: Jo…

JOANNA: I'm not going to drink it all if you help me.

KAREN: I really can't—I have to do some reading. I just found out I'm teaching a course on existentialism this fall. *(She goes to* JOANNA, *kisses her on the head.)* I'll see you in the morning.

*(*KAREN *exits.* RAY *sits down at the table.* JOANNA *comes over and sits on his lap.)*

JOANNA: I wish you'd be nice. She's going to think you want her to leave.

RAY: I do.

JOANNA: I don't. You're at work all the time, and I get lonely. I like having someone to talk to…someone to go get lunch with…

RAY: Can't you do that with your friends?

JOANNA: They're busy. They all have…jobs and… babies and stuff.

How was work?

RAY: All right.

JOANNA: What'd you do?—besides…take flowers off a dead guy?

RAY: The usual shit. Busted a drug deal…stopped a guy from beating up his wife…picked up a pervert.

*(Beat)*

JOANNA: A pervert?

What kind of pervert?

RAY: What do you mean, what kind of pervert?

JOANNA: I mean, what did he do?

RAY: Why do you want to know that?

JOANNA: I just—I like to hear about your job.

RAY: He'd been parking outside the high school, watching the girls' summer sports camps.

JOANNA: But that's not illegal. Is it?

RAY: No—not exactly. But it's creepy as hell. All those innocent girls playing soccer, or softball, and this old dude just sitting there staring at them. One of the moms figured out that he wasn't one of the dads and called the station.

JOANNA: So what'd you do?

RAY: Took him in for questioning. But we had to let him go, since he didn't have a record or anything.

JOANNA: Hmm.

RAY: What does hmm mean?

JOANNA: Hmm means…nothing. Hmm means…I'm glad you're home.

(JOANNA *begins kissing* RAY.)

RAY: Oh yeah?

(JOANNA *and* RAY *kiss.*)

JOANNA: Pookie?

RAY: Yeah?

JOANNA: What was the guy's name?

RAY: The pervert?

JOANNA: Yeah.

RAY: I don't know. Ian something. Ian…Madison—
Ian…Milton. Why?

JOANNA: No reason.

*(They continue kissing.)*

## Scene 2

*(JOANNA's kitchen. The next afternoon. KAREN is at the
table reading and taking notes. JOANNA enters, carrying
shopping bags.)*

JOANNA: Guess what?

KAREN: What?

JOANNA: I think I found someone!

KAREN: For what?

JOANNA: For you to meet!

KAREN: Oh, no. Is this somebody from that chat room?

JOANNA: No, it's somebody Ray arrested yesterday.
Or—not arrested—he took him in for questioning. But
listen—he didn't actually do anything.

KAREN: If he didn't do anything, then why did Ray
arrest him?

JOANNA: He didn't arrest him, he took him in for
questioning.

KAREN: Whatever.

JOANNA: He was watching…girls. Outside the high
school.

KAREN: Ew!

JOANNA: But that doesn't make him a criminal!

KAREN: I guess not, but it doesn't exactly make him a
catch!

JOANNA: You never know. He could be really great in other ways.

KAREN: Does Ray know you're trying to set me up with somebody he—

JOANNA: No!

KAREN: Then how did you find this guy?

JOANNA: Ray told me his name, and I stalked him on Facebook.

*(She opens the laptop and begins typing.)*

Let me show you his picture—he's really cute.

KAREN: No, I don't want to see his—oh, he is cute.

JOANNA: I told you. Ray said he doesn't have a record or anything. Plus, he has a really good job.

KAREN: What does he do?

JOANNA: He's a V P at an advertising agency over in Paulsboro. And he happened to mention on his profile that his favorite café is the Coffee Pot, and he eats lunch there practically every day.

KAREN: So?

JOANNA: So, you're going!

*(JOANNA picks up one of her shopping bags, which has a logo from a teen store like Mandee or Forever 21. From the bag she produces a ruffled mini-skirt and a sparkly Miley Cyrus T-shirt [depending on when and where the play is being performed, Miley Cyrus may be substituted for another young/teenage pop culture starlet.])*

JOANNA: And…you're wearing this.

KAREN: Oh my God.

JOANNA: Cute, right? Try it on!

KAREN: No.

JOANNA: Please?

KAREN: No!

JOANNA: Please please please? Just for fun?

KAREN: You really need a laugh this bad?

JOANNA: Don't you?
Come on. You know I'm going to beg you 'til you do it.

(KAREN *takes the bag and goes into the bedroom.* JOANNA *calls after her.*)

JOANNA: I spent three hours looking for the perfect thing at the mall this morning.

KAREN: *(Offstage)* Three hours?

JOANNA: Yeah. It was that or start drinking.

KAREN: *(Offstage)* You bought this *sober?*

JOANNA: I told you I was quitting today.

KAREN: *(Offstage)* I mean, that's good...but if you'd been drunk at least there'd be some excuse.

JOANNA: I don't know. I'm used to spending all this time at the hospital...wishing she'd just die already so I could have my life back...and now I do and it's like, what am I supposed to—

KAREN: *(Offstage)* You know, instead of tracking down pedophiles on the internet...you *could* get a job.

JOANNA: I have a job.

KAREN: *(Offstage)* Yeah, I know, but you're waitressing what—three shifts a week? I mean a real job.

JOANNA: If I had a real job I wouldn't be able to go into the city and audition.

KAREN: *(Offstage)* When was the last time you had an audition?

JOANNA: I've been busy with Mom, you know that.

(KAREN *reemerges in the outfit.* JOANNA *stares.*)

JOANNA: Wow.

KAREN: Can I take it off now?

JOANNA: You have really amazing legs. Has anyone ever told you that?

KAREN: No. But I don't think I've ever exposed this much of them.

JOANNA: You should. You look hot.

KAREN: I look like an idiot.

JOANNA: Yeah, okay, but a hot idiot. You're totally ready.

KAREN: For what?

JOANNA: Whatever happens when you go to the Coffee Pot.

KAREN: I'm not going to go to the Coffee Pot. I'm going to go take this thing off and finish my reading.

JOANNA: I really think you should go. This guy could be totally perfect for you.

KAREN: Even if he weren't a *pedophile*, Jo—I don't even live here.

JOANNA: Yeah, I know. But if you met somebody great then maybe you'd want to.
I mean, couldn't you work from anywhere? Isn't that sort of the point of teaching online?

KAREN: The point is my students can't see that I look younger than they do.

JOANNA: But you *could* work from anywhere.

KAREN: Yeah, I guess. But I like Chicago. I have an apartment. I have friends. I can't just up and move across the country.

JOANNA: Okay, well you could get a place here, and keep your place there too. Split time.

KAREN: That'd be really expensive.

JOANNA: We've got the life insurance money. What else are you going to do with it?

KAREN: I don't know. Buy a lot of shoes? What are you going to do with yours?

JOANNA: Actually, I've been thinking about that.

KAREN: Yeah?

JOANNA: I've been thinking it might be enough…for a wedding.

KAREN: A *wedding?* To Ray?

JOANNA: Look, I know you don't like him, but I love him.

KAREN: Okay…but you could love him without getting married.

JOANNA: But I want to get married.

KAREN: Why?

JOANNA: I don't know, everyone wants to get married.

KAREN: I don't. Or maybe I do, if I meet the right person—but maybe I don't.

JOANNA: Well, most people do. It's the happy ending.

KAREN: It isn't the "ending." If you get married now, you're going to live for—I don't know, fifty more years.

JOANNA: Maybe I'm not—Mom didn't.

KAREN: Maybe you're not, but you probably are. And do you really want to spend fifty more years with him?

JOANNA: Why not?

KAREN: He's not very…
He's kind of…

I just feel like you could do better.

JOANNA: Maybe when I was twenty-five I could have done better. But I'm thirty-six now. If I don't marry Ray…

KAREN: You'd meet someone else. You're still—

JOANNA: Maybe.

KAREN: Does he want to marry you?

JOANNA: Yeah.

KAREN: Have you asked him?

JOANNA: No. But I'm thinking I'll bring it up when he comes home this afternoon.

KAREN: This *afternoon?*

JOANNA: Yeah, he has the early shift today.

KAREN: You don't think you should take a little more time to think about it?

JOANNA: I've *been* thinking about it! I love him and he makes me happy. And just 'cause you don't have anybody who makes you happy doesn't mean you shouldn't be happy for me!

*(Beat)*

KAREN: Okay. I'll go out, then—I—I don't want to get in your way.

JOANNA: No, you don't have to—he won't even be home for a couple hours.

KAREN: Yeah, I—I need to get something to eat anyhow. I'll camp out at a coffee shop and do some reading.

JOANNA: Well, okay.

Which coffee shop?

KAREN: I usually go to Clyde's.

JOANNA: 'Cause you know…they have really good chicken sandwiches at the Coffee Pot. They use pesto, and arugula, and fresh mozzarella cheese.
It's almost two o'clock already—he probably won't even be there.

(KAREN *starts for the door.*)

KAREN: I'll see you later.

JOANNA: Wish me luck!

KAREN: Yeah. Good luck.

JOANNA: You too! It's on Ninth and Church Street, by the way. The Coffee Pot.

KAREN: I'm not going to go to the Coffee Pot! (*She exits, slamming the door behind her.*)


## Scene 3

(*The Coffee Pot.* KAREN *sits at a table. She is still wearing the mini-skirt and the Miley Cyrus t-shirt. She is finishing a sandwich and a cup of coffee and reading* Being and Nothingness.)

(IAN *enters, carrying a plate with a sandwich. He sits at a nearby table, takes a laptop out of his briefcase, and begins working and eating.* KAREN *looks up, recognizes him, then quickly looks down again. He looks at her, then looks away. She looks at him again, then looks away. They continue this game for a couple of minutes.*)

IAN: Excuse me.

(KAREN *jumps.*)

Sorry—I didn't mean to scare you.

KAREN: Um. It's okay.

IAN: What I wanted to ask was—I couldn't help noticing. Are you reading *Being and Nothingness*?

KAREN: Um. Yeah.

IAN: Really?

KAREN: Yeah.

IAN: That's...kind of amazing. When I was your age I was reading the Hardy Boys I think.

(KAREN *smiles*.)

IAN: So how do you like it?

KAREN: Um. It's okay.

IAN: Just okay?

KAREN: Yeah.

IAN: 'Cause, you know—Sartre was one of the most important philosophers of the twentieth century.

KAREN: Yeah, I—I know.
I just...don't necessarily agree with him.

IAN: Why not?

KAREN: Well...I like the concept of the origin of negation...but I'm skeptical of his take on conventional morality as a tool of the bourgeoisie. I kind of feel like morality derives from some set of universal standards, some concept of the essential good, rather than just being a way for the rich to control the rest of—

(KAREN *breaks off*. IAN *is staring at her*.)

IAN: Wow.

KAREN: What?

IAN: You've got quite a vocabulary.

KAREN: Oh—I, uh—

IAN: So what exactly do you mean by the essential good?

KAREN: I don't know. I think there's some kind of…
generally held consensus on what it means to be a
decent human being.

IAN: Sure, but different people are going to have
different opinions about that.

KAREN: Yeah, of course, but there are certain things we
all tend to agree on. You shouldn't kill, you shouldn't
rape, you shouldn't molest children— *(Suddenly
embarrassed)* —I mean—

IAN: But even those things change. Two or three
hundred years ago, murder was actually a pretty
standard way to settle disagreements.

KAREN: Sure, okay, but I like to think we're living in a
more enlightened time—

IAN: Really? When innocent people are dying and our
president wants to build a wall to keep them out?

KAREN: Well…

IAN: And the polar bears are starving and we can't
manage to stop driving our giant S U Vs? I think if
history has anything to teach us, it's that some of the
things that people think are all right now are going to
turn out to be wrong.

KAREN: Yeah, of course—standards are going to
change, with time—but that doesn't mean we
shouldn't have some—basic moral guidelines—

IAN: Yeah, maybe we should, but—

KAREN: I mean we can't be afraid to question them—

IAN: I think we have to consider ourselves obligated to
question them. Have you ever heard that quote?—"the
unexamined life is not worth living"?

KAREN: Yeah.

IAN: It's Ralph Waldo Emerson.

KAREN: I'm…pretty sure it's Socrates, actually.

IAN: Really? *(He types on the laptop.)* Yeah. You're right. Are you a…Miley Cyrus fan?

KAREN: What?

IAN: Your t-shirt.

KAREN: Oh. *(She looks down.)* Oh God! I…I left in a hurry, I forgot I had this on. I— no, I'm not. My, uh, my younger sister got it for me.

IAN: Oh.

KAREN: …Are you?

IAN: No. No, I'm afraid I'm not.

*(An awkward moment)*

IAN: Did you know that donkeys kill more people each year than plane crashes?

KAREN: Um. No. I didn't.

IAN: That's interesting, right?

KAREN: Yeah…

IAN: I work at this firm, this advertising firm, and we have a client right now—it's an oatmeal company, and they want to put a piece of trivia on each of their packets of oatmeal.

KAREN: I think that's a good one.

IAN: I don't know. It's kind of depressing. People might not want to think about death while they're eating breakfast. *(He looks at his screen.)* What about this? Some kinds of frogs can be frozen solid, then thawed, and go on living.

KAREN: I knew that, actually.

IAN: You did?

KAREN: Yeah. Back when I was in school—

IAN: Aren't you still in school?

KAREN: Um, well—not right now, 'cause—it's summer.
Anyway, the teacher brought in this case—like a
briefcase, with these gusts of liquid nitrogen coming
off of it—and there was this frog inside and he was
frozen—I mean there were ice crystals on his skin.
And she put him in a bowl of warm water for a few
minutes—and by the end of the class he was hopping
around like nothing had ever happened.

IAN: Wow.

KAREN: Yeah.

*(Beat)*

IAN: So I was just going to go…

KAREN: Oh. Okay. Bye.

IAN: *(Overlapping)* …get some more coffee. They have
free refills here.

KAREN: Oh.

IAN: Are you drinking coffee?—can I get you some?

KAREN: Okay.

(IAN *takes* KAREN'*s cup, then pauses.)*

IAN: How old are you, by the way?

KAREN: I'm, uh— *(She takes a deep breath.)* Fourteen.

IAN: Isn't it bad for someone your age to drink coffee?

KAREN: I…don't know. Is it?

IAN: I thought I heard it was.

KAREN: Maybe I'll just have to drink some more and
find out.

## Scene 4

*(The kitchen.* JOANNA *is taking cookies off an oven tray and arranging them on a plate. She hears keys in the lock. Suddenly nervous, she checks her hair and smoothes her apron.* RAY *enters.)*

JOANNA: Hey, pookie.

RAY: Hey, toots. *(Skeptical)* You made those?

JOANNA: Yeah. Well. I cut them up.

RAY: What are you wearing?

JOANNA: An apron. Do you like it?

RAY: It looks…weird. *(He crosses to the fridge and takes out a beer.)*

JOANNA: So, pookie?

RAY: Yeah?

JOANNA: I've been thinking about some things.

RAY: What kind of things?

JOANNA: Oh, you know. Things with us.

RAY: Oh yeah? How come?

JOANNA: I don't know. I guess 'cause my mom died. Didn't it make you think about things when your mom died?

RAY: *(Meditatively)* When my mom died I killed my neighbors' dog.

JOANNA: What?

RAY: Yeah.

JOANNA: Why?

RAY: I don't know. I was a kid, I was angry. It was stupid.

JOANNA: How did you—

RAY: My grandma called from the hospital—I'd just gotten home from baseball—and she told me. And I grabbed my keys and got in my car—it was a Datsun— beat-up old piece of shit. I didn't know where I was going but I wanted to drive somewhere. And our neighbors would just let the dog run around—and it was standing in the middle of the street, just standing there, looking up at a squirrel or something. And I saw it—way down the street, and—I didn't stop. Smashed the hell out of the fucker and kept on going.

*(Beat)*

JOANNA: I think maybe we should get married.

RAY: What?

Why do you want to get married?

JOANNA: I don't know. It just seems like it's time. We've been dating for almost two years—and we live together—

RAY: Well, maybe after I make detective—but toots, you know we can't afford a wedding right now.

JOANNA: No, but we can, because my mom left me that life insurance money. It wouldn't have to be anything fancy. We could do it in the church over on Crown Pointe Road. I could wear this dress I saw this morning at Macy's—it's silk, ivory silk, with a green sash, and we could have green and pink flowers. And then afterwards we could take pictures in Alcyon Park, and everyone walking by could look at us and smile because we'd look so happy.

*(RAY exits.)*

JOANNA: Where are you going?

RAY: *(Offstage)* Out.

JOANNA: Why?

RAY: *(Offstage)* Game's on. I'm gonna watch it down at McCoy's.

JOANNA: Watch it here.

RAY: *(Offstage)* I want a beer.

JOANNA: You're drinking a beer.

RAY: *(Re-entering, wearing jeans)* I want to go out.

*(RAY exits in the opposite direction. JOANNA looks after him, then pours herself some vodka and begins to drink.)*

## Scene 5

*(The kitchen. Evening. JOANNA is drinking and picking at the cookies. KAREN enters.)*

KAREN: Hi.

JOANNA: Where were you?

KAREN: Out, I was out—

JOANNA: I called you—

KAREN: I didn't have my ringer on. You're drinking?

JOANNA: I was worried about you! I called like five times and you didn't answer.

KAREN: I'm sorry.

JOANNA: Where were you?

KAREN: Um. All over really.

*(JOANNA waits.)*

First we were at the Coffee Pot, and then we went for a walk in that park—Alcyon Park—and then we sat on a bench and ate hot dogs like characters in a bad romantic comedy.

JOANNA: Whoa whoa whoa. You met him?

KAREN: Yeah.

JOANNA: And you were with him all afternoon?

KAREN: Yeah.

JOANNA: Didn't he have to work?

KAREN: He, um…he took the afternoon off.

JOANNA: You don't even like hot dogs.

KAREN: I know. But…today I did.

JOANNA: Did you have sex with him?

KAREN: No! It's not like that. At least I don't think it's like that.

JOANNA: Do you want it to be like that?

KAREN: No.
I don't know.

JOANNA: So what did you talk about?

KAREN: All kinds of stuff. Philosophy…politics…

JOANNA: Pedophilia?

KAREN: That isn't exactly "getting to know you" conversation.

JOANNA: It is if you're getting to know a pedophile.

KAREN: Well. We didn't.

JOANNA: Do you think you'll see him again?

KAREN: We're meeting for dinner tomorrow night.

JOANNA: Wow.

KAREN: I know.

JOANNA: So what did he say when you explained about Turner Syndrome?

KAREN: I, um…didn't.

JOANNA: You didn't.

Six hours of stimulating conversation, and you didn't manage to slip in the fact that you're thirty-eight years old?

KAREN: He thought I was...precocious.

JOANNA: I bet!

KAREN: I liked it.

JOANNA: Yeah, well, I'd like it if Ray thought I was a world champion, I don't know, tightrope walker—but I'm not.

KAREN: I know. I'll tell him at dinner tomorrow.

JOANNA: Good. 'Cause you know, if you didn't, and then you had sex with him—

KAREN: I'm not going to have sex with him!

JOANNA: Okay, but if you did—it'd be a crime. On his part.

KAREN: But I'm not really fourteen—

JOANNA: Doesn't matter, as long as he thinks you are. It's like when police officers pretend to be little kids in order to trap pedophiles on the internet. Ray's friend Lawrence did it one time.

KAREN: Oh my God, I almost forgot. Speaking of Ray...

JOANNA: What?

KAREN: Did you talk to him?

JOANNA: About what?

KAREN: Getting married.

JOANNA: Oh. Uh, no. I actually decided not to.

KAREN: Why?

JOANNA: I don't know. We can't really afford a wedding right now.

KAREN: Even with the life insurance?

JOANNA: I thought you'd be glad.

KAREN: Why?

JOANNA: 'Cause you don't think he's good enough for me.

KAREN: I shouldn't have said that. I'm sorry.

JOANNA: It's okay…

KAREN: I mean, like you said—he makes you happy, right?

JOANNA: Yeah.

KAREN: Then that's all that really matters.

JOANNA: Who are you and where have you put my sister?

(KAREN *smiles.*)

KAREN: I think I'm going to wear my hair in pigtails tomorrow night. Do you think my hair would look good in pigtails?


## Scene 6

(IAN *and* KAREN *at a nice restaurant. She is wearing her hair in pigtails. There is a birthday cake on the table between them.*)

IAN: Did that embarrass you? The waiters singing.

KAREN: Um…

IAN: It did, didn't it.

KAREN: Yeah.

IAN: I'm sorry.

KAREN: It's just…it's not my birthday.

IAN: I know.

KAREN: So…

IAN: I just thought it might look…strange. For a man—like me—to be here with a girl—like you. So I called ahead and told them I was taking my daughter out for her birthday.

KAREN: You told them you were my *dad?*

IAN: Yeah.

KAREN: That's kind of disturbing.

IAN: I didn't know they were going to sing. I'll tell them not to next time.

KAREN: Is it going to have to be my birthday every time we go out?

IAN: We'll always get a free dessert. You want some?

KAREN: No.

IAN: The thing is…you and I, spending time together… it could easily be misconstrued.

KAREN: What do you mean, misconstrued?

IAN: It means misinterpreted—taken the wrong way—

KAREN: I know what it means. I want to know what you mean by it.

IAN: I mean people could think this is something…you know, uh….
Which of course it's not.

*(Beat)*

KAREN: Where did our waiter go? Can we get the check?

IAN: Are you in a hurry?

KAREN: Yeah. I have some stuff to do tonight.

IAN: Got another date?

KAREN: This isn't a date.

IAN: No. It's not.

What just happened? Because we were having a good time. Weren't we?

KAREN: Yeah.

IAN: Was it the cake? We could order something different—

KAREN: No.

IAN: I really like spending time with you—you're… incredibly smart, and you're funny, and you're fun to be around—

KAREN: Okay, but you're not…

IAN: What?

KAREN: You're not attracted to me.

IAN: I—

KAREN: It's all right. Guys…usually aren't.

IAN: Actually, I can hardly look at you.

KAREN: Oh.

Wait, do you mean that in a good way or a bad way?

IAN: In a good way. Or…a bad way. Or a good way for you, but a bad way for me—what I mean is you're beautiful.

KAREN: I don't think anyone's ever said that to me before.

IAN: That's hard to believe.

KAREN: Usually people make me feel like…kind of a freak.

IAN: Kids can be cruel.

KAREN: Yeah. Adults can, too.

IAN: That's true.

KAREN: So you think I'm pretty?

IAN: I think you're—very pretty.

KAREN: Okay, but you don't think I'm—

IAN: What?

KAREN: You don't think I'm sexy.

IAN: I—

KAREN: It's okay. I don't think I am either.

IAN: I—I wish I didn't, but—

KAREN: Why?

IAN: Because you're fourteen.

KAREN: Oh. Right.
I have something I have to tell you, something I have to…explain.

IAN: Yeah—yeah. Me too.
You first.

KAREN: No—no, you first.

IAN: Okay.
Well—let me start at the beginning. Up until a year ago, I was married.

KAREN: Really?

IAN: Yeah.

KAREN: What happened?

IAN: She…was cheating on me. With one of her co-workers.

KAREN: That's awful.

IAN: Yeah. She was with him for three years and never told me. All the "work" dinners, drinks with "friends", "business" trips…I finally got a call from his wife, which was how I knew my marriage was over.

KAREN: I'm…sorry.

IAN: I met my wife when we were young—both sixteen—and once I met her I honestly never looked at anyone else. But then after the divorce—well, on my way home from work there's a high school. And I'd drive by it and see the girls' soccer teams practicing, and…one day I stopped and watched them for a while. It wasn't…a sexual thing—I don't know—it was confusing. They reminded me of her, when she was young, when we first met. And it made me feel better to watch them. And then I met you. And it makes me feel better to be with you—to talk to you—I feel like I've been frozen, and every time I see you another little piece of me thaws. First my feet, and then my calves, and then my knees, and then— *(He stops himself.)*

KAREN: And then?

IAN: That's, uh—that's as far as I've gotten.
I've gone out with a few women since my wife and I split up, and none of them have made me feel like you do.

KAREN: Why not?

IAN: I don't know…I feel like I can trust you. Maybe it's because you're young—but you just seem so…. Whenever I go out with a woman my own age, I can't help feeling like she's lying to me somehow. And of course she probably *is*—about how old she is, or the color of her hair, or how much she likes baseball— because that's what people do when they've first met. But I can't take it. After what happened with my wife, I just—can't take it. I don't want to be with a woman who's lying to me about anything.
So what was it you had to tell me?

KAREN: Oh. You know, I…don't even remember.

IAN: Must not have been very important.

KAREN: No, I…don't think it was.

*(Beat)*

IAN: Anyway...what I was trying to say is that I'm—very attracted to you, yeah. But.

KAREN: ...But what?

IAN: But I know that...doing anything about it would be terribly wrong.

KAREN: Then what are we doing here?

IAN: Talking.

KAREN: That's it?

IAN: Yeah.

*(An awkward silence)*

IAN: Did you know that Venus is the only planet which rotates clockwise?

KAREN: Huh.

*(Beat)*

IAN: How about this? Almost half of the weight of a six year old pillow is made up of dead skin cells and dust mites.

KAREN: Ew!

IAN: Yeah.

Or okay, here's a good one. Forty-year-old single women have better odds of being in a terrorist attack than they do of getting married.

KAREN: Yeah, I—I've heard that one.

We really should...just...get the check.

IAN: Okay.

*(IAN and KAREN look around for the waiter. Beat)*

KAREN: You know...I've had sex before.

IAN: *(Very surprised)* You have?

KAREN: Yeah.

IAN: With who?

KAREN: A guy. A couple of guys, actually.

IAN: Were they…your age?

KAREN: One was. But one was like thirty-five.

IAN: Really?

KAREN: Yeah.

*(Beat)*

IAN: Did you…like it?

KAREN: Yeah.
But I think I'd like it more with you.


## Scene 7

*(IAN's bedroom. IAN and KAREN sit on the edge of the bed, staring straight ahead, not touching.)*

KAREN: You're nervous.

IAN: Yeah. So are you.

KAREN: Yeah.

IAN: Aren't your parents going to wonder where you are?

KAREN: I haven't seen my dad in years. And my mom's dead.

IAN: Then who do you—

KAREN: She—sleeps like she's dead, I mean. She… won't even notice when I come in.

IAN: So your parents are divorced?

KAREN: Yeah.

IAN: I'm sorry.

KAREN: It's all right. It happened when I was young. Younger, I mean— 'cause I guess I'm still young.

IAN: Yeah.

Did you know that in Victorian England, having sex with a teenage girl was supposed to be a cure for sexually transmitted diseases?

KAREN: *(Pulling away)* Um.

IAN: Not that I have any! —It was just a piece of trivia—

KAREN: You definitely shouldn't put that one on the oatmeal packets!

IAN: Yeah—I—I know.

KAREN: You couldn't give me a piece of trivia about, I don't know, whales or something?

IAN: I could—of course I could—I'm sorry. Whales— let's see—did you know that blue whales used to be green? Really bright green, like grass, or stoplights?

KAREN: Really?

IAN: Yeah. Most of them turned blue, over time, because they blend in better with the water that way. But occasionally you'll still find green whales. They're terribly rare—and they, um, they can only mate with each other, so normally they'll swim around the ocean their entire lives looking for a mate and never find one. But every once in a while two green whales will find each other.

KAREN: That's amazing.

IAN: I made it up.

KAREN: What?

IAN: I don't know anything about whales. I'm sorry.

*(KAREN grabs a pillow, then stops.)*

KAREN: How old are these pillows?

IAN: Practically brand new.

*(KAREN hits IAN with the pillow. He grabs it and hits her back and they tussle for a moment, with her ending up on top of him. They look at each other, close, awkward. She kisses him. After a moment, he pulls away.)*

IAN: Was that okay?

KAREN: Yeah.

IAN: Are you sure?

KAREN: Yeah. Wasn't it?

IAN: Yeah.

KAREN: It was really okay, actually.

*(IAN and KAREN kiss again, he stops.)*

IAN: Was that okay?

KAREN: Really, *really* okay.

IAN: Are you sure?

KAREN: Yeah.

IAN and KAREN kiss again, he stops.)

IAN: How about that?

KAREN: Really, really, *really* okay.

IAN: Are you sure?

KAREN: Shhh. *(She leans in and begins kissing him again.)*

IAN: *(Pulling away)* But are you sure this is what you—

KAREN: Shhh.

*(IAN and KAREN continue kissing as the lights go down.)*

## Scene 8

*(The kitchen. It is late.* JOANNA *is drinking vodka in the dark.* RAY *enters from outside, stumbling a little.)*

RAY: You wanna know the best thing about being a cop?

*(*JOANNA *says nothing.)*

RAY: Nobody's ever gonna pull me over for drunk driving. It's a beautiful thing, drunk driving. Sorta like being on a carousel ride, the kind when you're little? And you get on the horse and the carousel starts and then it's going faster and faster and you know it's the same old world out there, but it's going so fast that it's all just color—and for those few minutes, while you're going around, you think maybe instead it's turned into something amazing.

And then you get off and you puke. *(He exits into the bedroom. A moment later, he returns, carrying a backpack filled with clothes.)*

JOANNA: Where are you going?

RAY: Kevin said I could stay at his place for a couple of days.

JOANNA: You're leaving?

RAY: I—

JOANNA: Fine. Leave. You know what I was just sitting here thinking?

RAY: What?

JOANNA: That sometimes I feel like I only fell in love with you because I got tired.

RAY: Yeah, well, sometimes I feel like I only fell in love with you 'cause you've got a nice ass.

JOANNA: Get out.

(RAY *exits.*)


# Scene 9

*(The next morning.* JOANNA *is sitting at the kitchen table, sobbing.* KAREN *enters from the guestroom.)*

KAREN: So I have to tell you about last night— *(She sees* JOANNA*)* What's wrong?

JOANNA: It's Ray. I—I don't know if we're going to make it.

KAREN: What happened?

JOANNA: He left.

KAREN: Where did he go?

JOANNA: I don't know!

KAREN: What did he say?

JOANNA: He said he was going to Kevin's.

KAREN: So he's at Kevin's.

JOANNA: Or he's at a bar picking up hookers!

KAREN: He's not picking up hookers.

JOANNA: How do you know?

KAREN: Because nobody picks up hookers at ten in the morning.

JOANNA: *(Sobbing harder)* You're supposed to say it's because he's in love with *me*!

KAREN: Of course he's in love with you. You're amazing.

JOANNA: I don't know. I'm kind of an alcoholic.

KAREN: Yeah, okay—but you're really great in other ways. Any guy would feel lucky to have you.

JOANNA: Mitch didn't. And Dave didn't. And Joey didn't, and Sam didn't—

KAREN: Well, yeah, but they were losers.

JOANNA: I know! I thought I'd finally found a guy who wasn't a loser! But I guess there's no such thing.

KAREN: That isn't true.

JOANNA: Are you talking about the pedophile?

KAREN: His name's Ian.

JOANNA: I know.

KAREN: And I'm not talking about him. Although we did have a really good date last night.

JOANNA: Did you tell him how old you are?

KAREN: Um. Yeah.

JOANNA: And he was okay with it.

KAREN: Yeah! He was totally fine.
You know what I've been thinking? I've been thinking about staying a little longer. Maybe even, I don't know, getting a place here.

JOANNA: You had sex with him, didn't you.

KAREN: No!

JOANNA: Yes you did.

KAREN: This isn't about him. I just—I was thinking about what you said. And you're right—there's no reason I couldn't try splitting time.

JOANNA: Just be careful, okay?

KAREN: You were the one that told me to go out with him in the first place.

JOANNA: I know…but I think I was wrong.

KAREN: I'm having a good time.

JOANNA: Sure you are, now, but he'll screw you over in the end. And I'm not just saying that 'cause he's a pedophile. They all screw you over in the end.

(RAY *enters.*)

RAY: Forgot my toothbrush. *(He exits into the bedroom.)*

JOANNA: He won't even talk to me!

KAREN: Yes he will. It's just 'cause I'm here. But as soon as I leave…

JOANNA: You don't have to go—

KAREN: I actually do. I'm meeting Ian for lunch.

JOANNA: Didn't you just see him yesterday?

KAREN: Yeah.

JOANNA: And the day before?

KAREN: Listen. You guys are going to be fine. He didn't come back here to get a toothbrush. You can buy a toothbrush for two dollars at Walgreens.

JOANNA: Yeah…

KAREN: He wants to talk to you.

JOANNA: You think so?

KAREN: Yeah.

JOANNA: Okay.

(KAREN *exits.* JOANNA *takes out a bottle of vodka, studies it, then puts it back in the cupboard quickly as* RAY *reenters.*)

RAY: She didn't have to leave.

JOANNA: She has a date.

RAY: *(Laughing)* With who?

JOANNA: This guy.

RAY: Is he some kind of pervert?

JOANNA: Why would you say that?

RAY: Cause he'd have to be some kind of pervert to be dating your sister.

JOANNA: He's not really dating her. They've only been out like twice. They haven't had sex or anything.

RAY: Hate to tell you this, babe, but most girls don't jump into bed on the second date. Of course, *some* girls jump into bed on the first date. If you can call getting a speeding ticket a first date.

JOANNA: You told me you loved that about me!

RAY: I did. You were this crazy thing—you did whatever you wanted. It was like everyone else was in black and white and you were in color.

JOANNA: That sounds like a line from a bad TV movie.

RAY: I think it is.

*(A moment)*

JOANNA: So now I'm not in color any more?

RAY: Now you want to get married…and then you'll want to get a house…and then pretty soon you'll want two point five kids and three fourths of a dog. And I… want to be by myself for a little while. *(He starts to exit.)*

JOANNA: Where are you going?

RAY: To work.

JOANNA: Are you coming back tonight?

RAY: I don't think so.

JOANNA: Can we talk about this?

RAY: I didn't come back to talk. I just came back to grab my toothbrush.

JOANNA: You can buy a toothbrush for two dollars at Walgreens!

RAY: Yeah, but I like this one. It fits my hand just right. *(He exits.)*

## Scene 10

*(The Coffee Pot.* IAN *and* KAREN *are having lunch.)*

IAN: And did you know that Eskimo languages have sixteen words for snow?

KAREN: Really?

IAN: Yeah—sixteen words, for all the different kinds of snow there are.

KAREN: I like that.

IAN: I do too.
I wish English were that precise, I think it would make it easier if there were words for all the complicated feelings that fall in between the feelings we understand.

KAREN: What do you mean?

IAN: I don't know what I'm doing here. With you. I mean, last night—it made me feel pretty great.

KAREN: Me too.

IAN: But it made me feel pretty awful, too.

KAREN: I'm sorry.

IAN: No, no, no—it's not your fault!

KAREN: But I wanted you to…

IAN: I know. But are you really old enough to know what you want?

KAREN: I don't know. Are you?

*(*JOANNA *enters, swaying slightly and drinking out of a flask.)*

JOANNA: He likes *that* toothbrush!

KAREN: Jo—uh—what are you doing?

JOANNA: He didn't come back to talk to me at all!

KAREN: Jo, I'm—

JOANNA: Can we please go get drunk? I know you're on a date—

IAN: *(Very nervous)* This isn't a date!

JOANNA: And I'm sorry to interrupt—and by the way, it's nice to meet you—but my boyfriend—ex-boyfriend—is a dickhead, and I really, really need to borrow my sister.

IAN: Sister?

JOANNA: You didn't tell him about me?

IAN: Karen mentioned a sister, but she said she was… younger.

JOANNA: Are you saying I look old? 'Cause that's the last thing I need right now—

KAREN: *(Standing, taking JOANNA's arm)* You know what, yeah, let's go, let's go somewhere—

IAN: Younger than her, I mean—

JOANNA: I am.

KAREN: Come on—we have to go—

IAN: Where are you going?

JOANNA: To a bar.

IAN: Karen can't go to a bar.

JOANNA: She just has to show them a letter from the doctor.

IAN: A letter from the doctor?

KAREN: Jo, stop.

IAN: Why do you have to show them a letter from the doctor?

JOANNA: You never told him.

*(KAREN shakes her head.)*

IAN: Told me what?

KAREN: Nothing.

JOANNA: You told me you told him.

IAN: *(To* KAREN*)* You told her about me?

KAREN: Yeah.

IAN: Oh, God.

KAREN: But it's okay! She's liberal—she's *really* liberal. Right?

(JOANNA *nods.)*

KAREN: She thinks it's fine.

JOANNA: I do! I think it's fine.

IAN: You think what I…am doing with her…is fine?

JOANNA: Yeah!

IAN: Um. Okay.
So…what haven't you told me?

KAREN: I…um…
I don't actually live here!

IAN: You don't?

KAREN: No. I grew up here…but I live in Chicago now. I was just here…helping out…'cause my mom was sick. But I might end up staying.

IAN: Okay…
But what does that have to do with bringing a letter from the doctor?

KAREN: Um, okay, well there was actually another thing.

IAN: What is it?

KAREN: I…I'm thirty-eight years old.

IAN: You're what?
Is this a joke?

KAREN: Sort of a cosmic joke, but, um, it's true.

IAN: But how—why do you look—

KAREN: I have a disease.

JOANNA: It's not a disease—

KAREN: It's called Turner Syndrome. It's a chromosome thing.

IAN: And it makes you look…like you're younger?

KAREN: It does different things to different people. But to me it does…this.

IAN: Then why did you tell me you were fourteen? — Why did you lie to me?

JOANNA: *(Trying to joke)* Come on, everyone lies about their age.

IAN: I thought I could trust you!

KAREN: I know—I—I thought it would make you like me better.

IAN: That's a terrible thing to think!

KAREN: I'm sorry.

IAN: I have to go.

KAREN: Can we talk about this?

IAN: I—I can't.

KAREN: I shouldn't have lied, but—

IAN: I have to go.

*(IAN exits. KAREN sits down heavily. JOANNA sits across from her. She pours vodka into KAREN's empty coffee cup, then pours some into IAN's cup for herself. They drink.)*

JOANNA: *(Trying to be cheerful)* You know what we should do?

KAREN: What?

JOANNA: We should get a place together! Now that I'm not with Ray, and you're not... whatever. It'd be just the two of us. It'd be fun.

KAREN: I—um...I don't know, Jo.

JOANNA: What do you mean? Why not?

KAREN: I might just...stay in Chicago.

JOANNA: You told me it wasn't about him.

KAREN: Yeah, I—I know, but now...

JOANNA: But now you want to stay in Chicago. How come you're totally willing to move across the country for some guy you just met, but not—

KAREN: I don't know, Jo. How come it always has to be about you?

JOANNA: It's not about me—

KAREN: It is, though. You're upset, so you have to come in all drunk in the middle of *my* date. Your boyfriend dumped you, so you have to give away all *my* secrets.

JOANNA: You think I *meant* to tell him?—

KAREN: I don't know. Did you?

JOANNA: No! You told me *you* told him! What were you thinking, anyway?

KAREN: I don't know! I—I wasn't thinking, I was just happy—

JOANNA: 'Cause I'm sorry, but that was stupid! I mean, you told me you were bad at dating—

KAREN: Me? What about you?

JOANNA: But did you think you could just go on forever with him thinking you were fourteen?

KAREN: No!

I—I knew it couldn't last. I just wanted it to last a little
longer. It was the first time I've ever been…really
happy, and I wanted it to last a little longer.

*(Beat)*

JOANNA: I'm sorry.

KAREN: No—I—I know you didn't mean to.

JOANNA: I'm still sorry.

KAREN: Okay.

JOANNA: Why couldn't you just tell him?

KAREN: Because I think he wants to be with a girl—not
a woman.

JOANNA: What a jerk.

KAREN: I know.

JOANNA: I think that's what Ray wants too.

KAREN: It's probably what all men want, one way or
another.

JOANNA: Yeah. That or they want to fuck their mothers.

KAREN: Yeah.

*(JOANNA and KAREN both drink.)*

JOANNA: I did talk to Ray. About getting married.

KAREN: And?

JOANNA: And…that's why he left.

KAREN: What an asshole.

JOANNA: I know.
Fuck them.

KAREN: Yeah. Fuck them.

*(JOANNA and KAREN both drink.)*

JOANNA: I'm never going to make it as an actress, am I.

KAREN: I don't know, Jo.

JOANNA: But you don't think I am. I know you don't.

KAREN: I—

JOANNA: It's okay. I don't think I am either. I was never very good, I was just pretty, and now I'm not even very pretty anymore.

KAREN: You're still—

JOANNA: Don't. I mean thank you, but don't.

KAREN: If you're not going to make it as an actress, then what are you going to do with your life?

JOANNA: I don't know. What are you going to do with your life?

KAREN: I don't know. Read books. Grade papers. Get older.

JOANNA: That's terrible.

KAREN: It's not that bad.
Okay, maybe it's kind of terrible. But it's better than feeling like this.

JOANNA: *(Starting to cry)* I miss Mom.

KAREN: You do?

JOANNA: Yeah. I think she was proud of us—I think she loved us—in her way, you know?

KAREN: I think she thought you were a slut, and I was a freak.

JOANNA: Yeah. But I mean…she was right. Wasn't she?

KAREN: Yeah.
I miss her too.

JOANNA: She was so tough. She was such a bitch, she was so tough, she was the toughest person I knew, and she died. She got sick, and she died, and if *she* died, then what hope is there for any of the rest of us?

KAREN: Not much.

(JOANNA *and* KAREN *drink.*)

JOANNA: If Ray leaves me I'm never going to quit drinking.

Who am I kidding. Whether or not Ray leaves me, I'm never going to quit drinking.

KAREN: I should tell you that's stupid. *(She pours herself more vodka.)*

JOANNA: Yeah. You should.


## Scene 11

(IAN *and* RAY *in a police interrogation room.* RAY *suddenly slams his fist down on the table.*)

RAY: Stupid!

IAN: I know.

RAY: We picked you up—what—three days ago?

IAN: Four.

RAY: Told you to stay away from teenage girls? And where do we find you not even a week later? Huh? Where'd we find you?

IAN: Outside the high school.

RAY: And what were you doing?

IAN: Watching...girls.
I know you're not going to believe me, but it wasn't a ...sexual thing. It just...made me feel better to watch them.

RAY: Oh yeah? And why's that? Their short shorts? Their smooth, hairless thighs?

IAN: No! Their...innocence. Their joy. This sounds pathetic.

I shouldn't have gone. I was having a really bad day.

RAY: Oh yeah? Some little prepubescent piece of ass turn you down?

IAN: No!

RAY: Then what happened?

IAN: None of your business.

RAY: *(Slamming his fist on the table again)* Answer the question!

IAN: I—I found out that the girl—the woman—I was seeing had been lying to me.

RAY: About what?

IAN: She had a…disease. And she hadn't told me.

RAY: What, like herpes?

IAN: No.

RAY: Chlamydia?

IAN: No!

RAY: Gonorrhea?

IAN: No!

RAY: 'Cause that's some nasty shit. Buddy of mine picked it up at a massage parlor and it almost made his balls fall off.

IAN: It's nothing like that—it's—it's something called Turner Syndrome.

RAY: Whoa, whoa, whoa. Karen Wilson?

IAN: Yeah…?

RAY: I'm dating her sister.

IAN: Oh! You're the dickhead.

(RAY *raises his fist.*)

RAY: Watch it, perv.

IAN: Sorry. I—I met your girlfriend today.

RAY: You did?

IAN: Yeah.

RAY: How'd she—how'd she look?

IAN: Is this part of the investigation?

RAY: Answer the question, pervoid.

IAN: She looked pretty upset.

RAY: She did?

IAN: Yeah. What'd you do?

RAY: None of your business.
So you're the guy Karen was seeing.

IAN: I—

RAY: And you didn't know about Turner's—which means you thought she was a teenage girl, didn't you!

IAN: No!

RAY: I knew she was dating a pervert!

IAN: I didn't know about the disease, but I—I knew how old she was, the whole time.

RAY: Oh, yeah? *(He takes out a cell phone, dials.)*
Karen? It's Ray. *(Beat. He looks at the phone.)* Shit. *(He dials again.)* Don't hang up. I'm gonna need you to come down to the station and answer a couple of questions.
Ian Milton. We caught him watching girls down at the high school.
Well, I'm sorry, but I'm not asking.
If you're not down here in about two minutes, I'm gonna have to send a squad car and have you arrested for obstruction.
Good. See you soon. *(He hangs up.)* Nervous?

IAN: *(Nervous)* No.

RAY: We're gonna get you for intent to seduce a minor. You know what the penalty is for that? Couple of years.

IAN: She isn't a minor.

RAY: Doesn't matter, as long as you thought she was. You'll be fine, though. You got a cute little butt. I bet you'll make lots of friends.

(IAN *and* RAY *sit in silence for a moment.*)

RAY: So…uh…what'd Joanna say about me?

IAN: Just that you're a dickhead.

RAY: That's it?

IAN: Yeah.
You're doing pretty well for yourself.

RAY: What do you mean?

IAN: She's cute.

RAY: I don't need a pervert to tell me that.
I thought you only liked girls who weren't legal yet.

IAN: You thought wrong. I was married for almost twenty years.

RAY: Really?

IAN: Yeah.

RAY: How'd you like it?

IAN: Being married? What does that have to do with—

RAY: Just answer the question, pervalicious.

IAN: It was great.

RAY: Yeah?

IAN: Yeah, for a while, and then it all fell apart.

(A *knock on the door.*)

RAY: Come on in.

(KAREN *enters.*)

KAREN: Tell me what you want and let me go home.

RAY: You know this guy?

KAREN: Yeah.

RAY: How?

KAREN: We, uh—we went out a few times.

RAY: Are you still going out?

KAREN: No.

RAY: Why not?

KAREN: Because he's an asshole.

IAN: I'm not an—

RAY: Zip it, Pervy McPerverson. (*To* KAREN) While you were going out…did he attempt to seduce you?

KAREN: Yeah.

RAY: And did he succeed?

(*Beat*)

KAREN: Yeah.

RAY: And at that time, did he think you were a minor?

(*Long pause.* KAREN *looks at* IAN)

KAREN: No. He knew how old I was from the beginning.

RAY: (*Surprised*) He did?

KAREN: Yeah.

RAY: Really?

KAREN: Uh-huh.

RAY: But if he didn't know about Turner's— (*To* IAN) Then what exactly did you think was going on with her?

IAN: I, uh, I thought she just looked…really amazing for her age. For any age. I thought she just looked really amazing.

RAY: *(Skeptical)* Uh-huh.

KAREN: Can I go now?

RAY: Yeah.

*(KAREN starts to exit.)*

IAN: Karen, wait. Can we talk? Can we go somewhere and have a cup of coffee?

KAREN: I think it's probably bad for someone my age to drink coffee. *(She exits.)*

RAY: I've gotta tell you, man, I don't get it.

IAN: What?

RAY: If it wasn't the pervert thing, then what did you see in her?

IAN: We just had a connection. It was like everyone else was in black and white and she was in color.

RAY: *(Startled)* Where did you get that line?

IAN: I think I heard it in a bad T V movie.

RAY: Huh.

*(Beat)*

IAN: So…you can't charge me with anything?

RAY: If you get within five hundred yards of the high school again we can. But for now, you're free to go.

*(IAN starts to exit.)*

RAY: Hey. Let me ask you one more thing.

IAN: I thought I was free to go.

RAY: Yeah…you are. You are. I was just wondering.

IAN: Okay…

RAY: 'Cause—my parents weren't married. And most of my buddies aren't married—haven't ever been married—and I ask them about getting married and they say it's not worth it, you know, you've gotta feel like an asshole every time you go to a strip club, and then most likely it doesn't last anyhow. But…they haven't been married, so what do they know? And… you've been married, and it didn't last, and most likely it doesn't, but… *(He trails off.)*

IAN: What's the question?

RAY: Maybe it's worth it anyhow?

IAN: I think it's worth it if you meet the right woman.

RAY: But how do you know if it's the right woman?

IAN: Because she's everything you never knew you always wanted.

RAY: Is that from a bad T V movie too?

IAN: I think so.

RAY: It's a pretty good line.

IAN: It is, isn't it.

## Scene 12

*(The Coffee Pot. IAN sits at a table. KAREN enters.)*

IAN: Thank you for coming.

KAREN: It was the only way I could think of to get you to stop calling me.

IAN: That's it?

*(Beat)*

KAREN: The thing you said, about the sixteen words for snow.

IAN: Yeah?

KAREN: I looked that up, because I liked it, and I thought—I don't know what I thought. But you know what I found out?

IAN: What?

KAREN: They're basically all the same word. See, Eskimo languages are polysynthetic—which means that something that would be a phrase in English, they turn it into a single compound word. So they've got a root word that means snow, and then they add different endings onto it, but it's actually just the same as us saying dirty snow, or sparkly snow, or whatever. So whoever came up with that piece of trivia, that they had sixteen words for snow, was really just trying to trick us, to make us think they were a little more precise, had things a little more figured out than we did.

IAN: I'll make sure not to put that one on the oatmeal packets, then.

KAREN: Yeah. You should.

*(Beat)*

IAN: So I wanted to thank you for what you said down at the station.

KAREN: Okay.
That's it?

IAN: And I wanted to ask you if this—this thing between us—if—maybe we could try it again. Now that everything's out in the open. If maybe we could see if it could work.

*(Beat)*

KAREN: I don't think so. You've obviously got some trust issues.

IAN: Yeah.

KAREN: And some pedophilia issues.

IAN: I...I was confused.

KAREN: No—you weren't just confused, you were scared. You couldn't deal with being with anyone who might *ever* do what your wife did. And I'm sorry about what your wife did, but you know what? It happens. People pick you up and then they put you back down and then they get in a steamroller and they roll over you, and then you know what they do? They put it in reverse and they go right back and do it again!

IAN: Okay, fine, but you were scared too! You were too scared of being rejected to tell me the truth.

KAREN: You couldn't have handled it!

IAN: How do you know? You couldn't even let me try, because you've got a massive inferiority complex! You're smart and you're funny and you're gorgeous— you are! —But you don't know it, any of it, because you've got this thing—

KAREN: This disease!—

IAN: Sure, but everybody's got a disease, one way or another!

*(Beat)*

KAREN: I just—think it'd be best—if we didn't see each other anymore.

*(Beat)*

IAN: Okay.

*(Beat)*

KAREN: But.

IAN: ...But what?

KAREN: But I really, really want to kiss you right now.

IAN: You do?

KAREN: Yeah.

IAN: I really, really want to kiss you right now too.

KAREN: You do?

IAN: Yeah.

KAREN: Then come here.

IAN: Okay.

(IAN *crosses to* KAREN *and they kiss.*)

IAN: I also really, really want to kiss you tomorrow. And the next day. And the next day.

KAREN: And the day after that?

IAN: I don't know. I might get sick of you by then.

KAREN: Not if I get sick of you first.

(IAN *and* KAREN *continue kissing.*)

## Scene 13

(JOANNA's *kitchen.* JOANNA *is drinking vodka out of a teacup in her pajamas.* RAY *enters, holding his bags. She looks up.*)

RAY: Hi.

JOANNA: Hi.

RAY: What are you doing in your pajamas?

(JOANNA *shrugs.*)

RAY: It's three P M.

JOANNA: Yeah.

RAY: Are you okay?

JOANNA: I don't know.

RAY: Hold on.

(RAY *exits into the bedroom.* JOANNA *drinks more vodka. He reenters in his pajamas. He takes a teacup out of the cupboard and sits down at the table.)*

RAY: Can I have some?

(JOANNA *passes* RAY *the bottle. He pours some into a teacup and drinks. After a moment)*

RAY: Maybe we should get married.

JOANNA: Really?

RAY: Yeah.

JOANNA: Why?

RAY: Because you're everything I never knew I always wanted.

JOANNA: Is that from a bad T V movie?

RAY: Yeah.

What do you think?

JOANNA: Okay.


## Scene 14

(JOANNA's *kitchen.* JOANNA *sits at the kitchen table, flipping through a bridal magazine.* KAREN *enters.)*

JOANNA: Hi.

KAREN: Hi.

JOANNA: How are you?

KAREN: I'm okay. How are you?

JOANNA: I'm okay. I have something to tell you.

KAREN: Yeah?

JOANNA: I'm back with Ray.

KAREN: Really?

JOANNA: Yeah. He came home. And…we're getting married.

(*Beat*)

KAREN: Jo…I mean, you said it yourself—he's kind of a dickhead.

JOANNA: I know. But he's really great in other ways.

KAREN: Okay…

JOANNA: I mean, he's not perfect—but neither am I. And we make each other happy.

KAREN: Do you?

JOANNA: Yeah. Or—I don't know—probably happier than we would be alone.
Will you be my maid of honor?

KAREN: Yeah—yeah. Of course.

JOANNA: I'm thinking green. For the dresses.

KAREN: I like green.

JOANNA: Good.

KAREN: I have something to tell you too.

JOANNA: Yeah?

KAREN: I'm back with Ian.

JOANNA: Really?

KAREN: Yeah…we met up for lunch, and…

JOANNA: You worked some things out?

KAREN: Well…no, not really. We just kind of made out for a while. But we want to try.

JOANNA: So you're going to stay here?

KAREN: Yeah—for a while at least—I'll look for a sublet for the summer. And then maybe in the fall I'll get a place. Or…maybe he'll move to Chicago. I don't know. It's early. We'll see how it goes.

JOANNA: Okay.
I'd like to get to know him. We should all have dinner together.

KAREN: ...You think?

JOANNA: Yeah. You and him, me and Ray...

KAREN: You don't think that'd be...

JOANNA: No. I think it'd be great.

KAREN: Okay...

JOANNA: Maybe tomorrow?

KAREN: I'll ask him.

JOANNA: We could get a lasagna. Does he like lasagna?

KAREN: Everyone likes lasagna.

JOANNA: That's true. And maybe he could bring over a bottle of wine. Or...four.

KAREN: Sure.

*(Beat)*

JOANNA: Do you think we're being stupid? I mean, really, really stupid?

KAREN: I think everybody who loves somebody else is being really, really stupid.

JOANNA: But do you think it's worth it?

KAREN: I don't know. What do you think?

*(The lights linger on JOANNA and KAREN for a moment before JOANNA answers, then go down.)*

END OF PLAY